Apology
Also known as The Death of Socrates

Plato

Translated by Benjamin Jowett

Contents

INTRODUCTION. 7
APOLOGY by Plato Translated by Benjamin Jowett 18

APOLOGY
ALSO KNOWN AS THE
DEATH OF SOCRATES

BY
Plato

Translated by Benjamin Jowett

INTRODUCTION.

In what relation the Apology of Plato stands to the real defence of Socrates, there are no means of determining. It certainly agrees in tone and character with the description of Xenophon, who says in the Memorabilia that Socrates might have been acquitted 'if in any moderate degree he would have conciliated the favour of the dicasts;' and who informs us in another passage, on the testimony of Hermogenes, the friend of Socrates, that he had no wish to live; and that the divine sign refused to allow him to prepare a defence, and also that Socrates himself declared this to be unnecessary, on the ground that all his life long he had been preparing against that hour. For the speech breathes throughout a spirit of defiance, (ut non supplex aut reus sed magister aut dominus videretur esse judicum' (Cic. de Orat.); and the loose and desultory style is an imitation of the 'accustomed manner' in which Socrates spoke in 'the agora and among the tables of the money-changers.' The allusion in the Crito may, perhaps, be adduced as a further evidence of the literal accuracy of some parts. But in the main it must be regarded as the ideal of Socrates, according to Plato's conception of him, appearing in the greatest and most public scene of his life, and in the height of his triumph, when he is weakest, and yet his mastery over mankind is greatest, and his habitual irony acquires a new meaning and a sort of tragic pathos in the face of death. The facts of his life are summed up, and the features of his character are brought out as if by accident in the course of the defence. The conversational manner, the seeming want of arrangement, the ironical simplicity, are found to result in a perfect work of art, which is the portrait of Socrates.

Yet some of the topics may have been actually used by Socrates; and the recollection of his very words may have rung in the ears of his disciple. The Apology of Plato may be compared generally with those speeches of Thucydides in which he has embodied his conception of the lofty character and policy of the great Pericles, and which at the same time furnish a commentary on the situation of affairs from the point of view of the historian. So in the Apology there is an ideal rather than a literal truth; much is said which was not said, and is only Plato's view of the situation. Plato was not, like Xenophon, a chronicler of facts; he does not appear in any of his writings to have aimed at literal accuracy. He is not therefore to be supplemented from the Memorabilia and Symposium of Xenophon, who belongs to an entirely different class of writers. The Apology of Plato is not the report of what Socrates said, but an elaborate composition, quite as much so in fact as one of the Dialogues. And we may perhaps even indulge in the fancy that the actual defence of Socrates was as much greater than the Platonic defence as the master was greater than the disciple. But in any case, some of the words used by him must have been remembered, and some of the facts recorded must have actually occurred. It is significant that Plato is said to have been present at the defence (Apol.), as he is also said to have been absent at the last scene in the Phaedo. Is it fanciful to suppose that he meant to give the stamp of authenticity to the one and not to the other?--especially when we consider that these two passages are the only ones in which Plato makes mention of himself. The circumstance that Plato was to be one of his sureties for the payment of the fine which he proposed has the appearance of truth. More suspicious is the statement that Socrates received the first impulse to his favourite calling of cross-examining the world from the Oracle of Delphi; for he must already have been famous before Chaerephon went to consult the Oracle (Riddell), and the story is of a kind which is very likely to have been invented. On the whole we arrive at the conclusion that the Apology is true to the character of Socrates, but we cannot show that any single sentence in it was actually spoken by him. It breathes the spirit of Socrates, but has been cast anew in the mould of Plato.

There is not much in the other Dialogues which can be compared with the Apology. The same recollection of his master may have been present to the mind of Plato when depicting the sufferings of the Just in the Republic. The Crito may also be regarded as a sort of appendage to the Apology, in which Socrates, who has defied the judges, is nevertheless represented as scrupulously obedient to the laws. The idealization of the sufferer is carried still further in the Gorgias, in which the thesis is maintained, that 'to suffer is better than to do evil;' and the art of rhetoric is described as only useful for the purpose of self-accusation. The parallelisms which occur in the so-called Apology of Xenophon are not worth noticing, because the writing in which they are contained is manifestly spurious. The statements of the Memorabilia respecting the trial and death of Socrates agree generally with Plato; but they have lost the flavour of Socratic irony in the narrative of Xenophon.

The Apology or Platonic defence of Socrates is divided into three parts: 1st. The defence properly so called; 2nd. The shorter address in mitigation of the penalty; 3rd. The last words of prophetic rebuke and exhortation.

The first part commences with an apology for his colloquial style; he is, as he has always been, the enemy of rhetoric, and knows of no rhetoric but truth; he will not falsify his character by making a speech. Then he proceeds to divide his accusers into two classes; first, there is the nameless accuser--public opinion. All the world from their earliest years had heard that he was a corrupter of youth, and had seen him caricatured in the Clouds of Aristophanes. Secondly, there are the professed accusers, who are but the mouth-piece of the others. The accusations of both might be summed up in a formula. The first say, 'Socrates is an evil-doer and a curious person, searching into things under the earth and above the heaven; and making the worse appear the better cause, and teaching all this to others.' The second, 'Socrates is an evil-doer and corrupter of the youth, who does not receive the gods whom the state receives, but introduces other new divinities.' These last words appear to have been the actual indictment (compare Xen. Mem.); and the previous formula, which is a summary of public opinion, assumes the same legal style.

The answer begins by clearing up a confusion. In the representations of the Comic poets, and in the opinion of the multitude, he had been identified with the teachers of physical science and with the Sophists. But this was an error. For both of them he professes a respect in the open court, which contrasts with his manner of speaking about them in other places. (Compare for Anaxagoras, Phaedo, Laws; for the Sophists, Meno, Republic, Tim., Theaet., Soph., etc.) But at the same time he shows that he is not one of them. Of natural philosophy he knows nothing; not that he despises such pursuits, but the fact is that he is ignorant of them, and never says a word about them. Nor is he paid for giving instruction--that is another mistaken notion:--he has nothing to teach. But he commends Evenus for teaching virtue at such a 'moderate' rate as five minae. Something of the 'accustomed irony,' which may perhaps be expected to sleep in the ear of the multitude, is lurking here.

He then goes on to explain the reason why he is in such an evil name. That had arisen out of a peculiar mission which he had taken upon himself. The enthusiastic Chaerephon (probably in anticipation of the answer which he received) had gone to Delphi and asked the oracle if there was any man wiser than Socrates; and the answer was, that there was no man wiser. What could be the meaning of this--that he who knew nothing, and knew that he knew nothing, should be declared by the oracle to be the wisest of men? Reflecting upon the answer, he determined to refute it by finding 'a wiser;' and first he went to the politicians, and then to the poets, and then to the craftsmen, but always with the same result--he found that they knew nothing, or hardly anything more than himself; and that the little advantage which in some cases they possessed was more than counter-balanced by their conceit of knowledge. He knew nothing, and knew that he knew nothing: they knew little or nothing, and imagined that they knew all things. Thus he had passed his life as a sort of missionary in detecting the pretended wisdom of mankind; and this occupation had quite absorbed him and taken him away both from public and private affairs. Young men of the richer sort had made a pastime of the same pursuit, 'which was not unamusing.' And hence bitter enmities had arisen; the professors of knowledge had revenged themselves by calling him a villainous corrupter of youth, and by repeating the commonplaces about atheism and materialism and sophistry, which are the stock-accusations against all philosophers when there is nothing else to be said of them.

The second accusation he meets by interrogating Meletus, who is present and can be interrogated. 'If he is the corrupter, who is the improver of the citizens?' (Compare Meno.) 'All men everywhere.' But how absurd, how contrary to analogy is this! How inconceivable too, that he should make the citizens worse when he has to live with them. This surely cannot be intentional; and if unintentional, he ought to have been instructed by Meletus, and not accused in the court.

But there is another part of the indictment which says that he teaches men not to receive the gods whom the city receives, and has other new gods. 'Is that the way in which he is supposed to corrupt the youth?' 'Yes, it is.' 'Has he only new gods, or none at all?' 'None at all.' 'What, not even the sun and moon?' 'No; why, he says that the sun is a stone, and the moon earth.' That, replies Socrates, is the old confusion about Anaxagoras; the Athenian people are not so ignorant as to attribute to the influence of Socrates notions which have found their way into the drama, and may be learned at the theatre. Socrates undertakes to show that Meletus (rather unjustifiably) has been compounding a riddle in this part of the indictment: 'There are no gods, but Socrates believes in the existence of the sons of gods, which is absurd.'

Leaving Meletus, who has had enough words spent upon him, he returns to the original accusation. The question may be asked, Why will he persist in following a profession which leads him to death? Why?--because he must remain at his post where the god has placed him, as he remained at Potidaea, and Amphipolis, and Delium, where the generals placed him. Besides, he is not so overwise as to imagine that he knows whether death is a good or an evil; and he is certain that desertion of his duty is an evil. Anytus is quite right in saying that they should never have indicted him if they meant to let him go. For he will certainly obey God rather than man; and will continue to preach to all men of all ages the necessity of virtue and improvement; and if they refuse to listen to him he will still persevere and reprove them. This is his way of corrupting the youth, which he will not cease to follow in obedience to the god, even if a thousand deaths await him.

He is desirous that they should let him live--not for his own sake, but for theirs; because he is their heaven-sent friend (and they will never have such another), or, as he may be ludicrously described, he is the gadfly who stirs the generous steed into motion. Why then has he never taken part in public affairs? Because the familiar divine voice has hindered him; if he had been a public man, and had fought for the right, as he would certainly have fought against the many, he would not have lived, and could therefore have done no good. Twice in public matters he has risked his life for the sake of justice--once at the trial of the generals; and again in resistance to the tyrannical commands of the Thirty.

But, though not a public man, he has passed his days in instructing the citizens without fee or reward--this was his mission. Whether his disciples have turned out well or ill, he cannot justly be charged with the result, for he never promised to teach them anything. They might come if they liked, and they might stay away if they liked: and they did come, because they found an amusement in hearing the pretenders to wisdom detected. If they have been corrupted, their elder relatives (if not themselves) might surely come into court and witness against him, and there is an opportunity still for them to appear. But their fathers and brothers all appear in court (including 'this' Plato), to witness on his behalf; and if their relatives are corrupted, at least they are uncorrupted; 'and they are my witnesses. For they know that I am speaking the truth, and that Meletus is lying.'

This is about all that he has to say. He will not entreat the judges to spare his life; neither will he present a spectacle of weeping children, although he, too, is not made of 'rock or oak.' Some of the judges themselves may have complied with this practice on similar occasions, and he trusts that they will not be angry with him for not following their example. But he feels that such conduct brings discredit on the name of Athens: he feels too, that the judge has sworn not to give away justice; and he cannot be guilty of the impiety of asking the judge to break his oath, when he is himself being tried for impiety.

As he expected, and probably intended, he is convicted. And now the tone of the speech, instead of being more conciliatory, becomes more lofty and commanding. Anytus proposes death as the penalty: and what counter-proposition shall he make? He, the benefactor of the Athenian people, whose whole life has been spent in doing them good, should at least have the Olympic victor's reward of maintenance in the Prytaneum. Or why should he propose any counter-penalty when he does not know whether death, which Anytus proposes, is a good or an evil? And he is certain that imprisonment is an evil, exile is an evil. Loss of money might be an evil, but then he has none to give; perhaps he can make up a mina. Let that be the penalty, or, if his friends wish, thirty minae; for which they will be excellent securities.

(He is condemned to death.)

He is an old man already, and the Athenians will gain nothing but disgrace by depriving him of a few years of life. Perhaps he could have escaped, if he had chosen to throw down his arms and entreat for his life. But he does not at all repent of the manner of his defence; he would rather die in his own fashion than live in theirs. For the penalty of unrighteousness is swifter than death; that penalty has already overtaken his accusers as death will soon overtake him.

And now, as one who is about to die, he will prophesy to them. They have put him to death in order to escape the necessity of giving an account of their lives.

But his death 'will be the seed' of many disciples who will convince them of their evil ways, and will come forth to reprove them in harsher terms, because they are younger and more inconsiderate.

He would like to say a few words, while there is time, to those who would have acquitted him. He wishes them to know that the divine sign never interrupted him in the course of his defence; the reason of which, as he conjectures, is that the death to which he is going is a good and not an evil. For either death is a long sleep, the best of sleeps, or a journey to another world in which the souls of the dead are gathered together, and in which there may be a hope of seeing the heroes of old--in which, too, there are just judges; and as all are immortal, there can be no fear of any one suffering death for his opinions.

Nothing evil can happen to the good man either in life or death, and his own death has been permitted by the gods, because it was better for him to depart; and therefore he forgives his judges because they have done him no harm, although they never meant to do him any good.

He has a last request to make to them--that they will trouble his sons as he has troubled them, if they appear to prefer riches to virtue, or to think themselves something when they are nothing.

...

'Few persons will be found to wish that Socrates should have defended himself otherwise,'--if, as we must add, his defence was that with which Plato has provided him. But leaving this question, which does not admit of a precise solution, we may go on to ask what was the impression which Plato in the Apology intended to give of the character and conduct of his master in the last great scene? Did he intend to represent him (1) as employing sophistries; (2) as designedly irritating the judges? Or are these sophistries to be regarded as belonging to the age in which he lived and to his personal character, and this apparent haughtiness as flowing from the natural elevation of his position?

For example, when he says that it is absurd to suppose that one man is the corrupter and all the rest of the world the improvers of the youth; or, when he argues that he never could have corrupted the men with whom he had to live; or, when he proves his belief in the gods because he believes in the sons of gods, is he serious or jesting? It may be observed that these sophisms all occur in his cross-examination of Meletus, who is easily foiled and mastered in the hands of the great dialectician. Perhaps he regarded these answers as good enough for his accuser, of whom he makes very light. Also there is a touch of irony in them, which takes them out of the category of sophistry. (Compare Euthyph.)

That the manner in which he defends himself about the lives of his disciples is not satisfactory, can hardly be denied. Fresh in the memory of the Athenians, and detestable as they deserved to be to the newly restored democracy, were the names of Alcibiades, Critias, Charmides. It is obviously not a sufficient answer that Socrates had never professed to teach them anything, and is therefore not justly chargeable with their crimes. Yet the defence, when taken out of this ironical form, is doubtless sound: that his teaching had nothing to do with their evil lives. Here, then, the sophistry is rather in form than in substance, though we might desire that to such a serious charge Socrates had given a more serious answer.

Truly characteristic of Socrates is another point in his answer, which may also be regarded as sophistical. He says that 'if he has corrupted the youth, he must have corrupted them involuntarily.' But if, as Socrates argues, all evil is involuntary, then all criminals ought to be admonished and not punished. In these words the Socratic doctrine of the involuntariness of evil is clearly intended to be conveyed. Here again, as in the former instance, the defence of Socrates is untrue practically, but may be true in some ideal or transcendental sense. The commonplace reply, that if he had been guilty of corrupting the youth their relations would surely have witnessed against him, with which he concludes this part of his defence, is more satisfactory.

Again, when Socrates argues that he must believe in the gods because he believes in the sons of gods, we must remember that this is a refutation not of the original indictment, which is consistent enough--'Socrates does not receive the gods whom the city receives, and has other new divinities' --but of the interpretation put upon the words by Meletus, who has affirmed that he is a downright atheist. To this Socrates fairly answers, in accordance with the ideas of the time, that a downright atheist cannot believe in the sons of gods or in divine things. The notion that demons or lesser divinities are the sons of gods is not to be regarded as ironical or sceptical. He is arguing 'ad hominem' according to the notions of mythology current in his age. Yet he abstains from saying that he believed in the gods whom the State approved. He does not defend himself, as Xenophon has defended him, by appealing to his practice of religion. Probably he neither wholly believed, nor disbelieved, in the existence of the popular gods; he had no means of knowing about them. According to Plato (compare Phaedo; Symp.), as well as Xenophon (Memor.), he was punctual in the performance of the least religious duties; and he must have believed in his own oracular sign, of which he seemed to have an internal witness. But the existence of Apollo or Zeus, or the other gods whom the State approves, would have appeared to him both uncertain and unimportant in comparison of the duty of self-examination, and of those principles of truth and right which he deemed to be the foundation of religion. (Compare Phaedr.; Euthyph.; Republic.)

The second question, whether Plato meant to represent Socrates as braving or irritating his judges, must also be answered in the negative. His irony, his superiority, his audacity, 'regarding not the person of man,' necessarily flow out of the loftiness of his situation. He is not acting a part upon a great occasion, but he is what he has been all his life long, 'a king of men.' He would rather not appear insolent, if he could avoid it (ouch os authadizomenos touto lego). Neither is he desirous of hastening his own end, for life and death are simply indifferent to him. But such a defence as would be acceptable to his judges and might procure an acquittal, it is not in his nature to make. He will not say or do anything that might pervert the course of justice; he cannot have his tongue bound even 'in the throat of death.' With his accusers he will only fence and play, as he had fenced with other 'improvers of youth,' answering the Sophist according to his sophistry all his life long. He is serious when he is speaking of his own mission, which seems to distinguish him from all other reformers of mankind, and originates in an accident. The dedication of himself to the improvement of his fellow-citizens is not so remarkable as the ironical spirit in which he goes about doing good only in vindication of the credit of the oracle, and in the vain hope of finding a wiser man than himself. Yet this singular and almost accidental character of his mission agrees with the divine sign which, according to our notions, is equally accidental and irrational, and is nevertheless accepted by him as the guiding principle of his life. Socrates is nowhere represented to us as a freethinker or sceptic. There is no reason to doubt his sincerity when he speculates on the possibility of seeing and knowing the heroes of the Trojan war in another world. On the other hand, his hope of immortality is uncertain;--he also conceives of death as a long sleep (in this respect differing from the Phaedo), and at last falls back on resignation to the divine will, and the certainty that no evil can happen to the good man either in life or death. His absolute truthfulness seems to hinder him from asserting positively more than this; and he makes no attempt to veil his ignorance in mythology and figures of speech. The gentleness of the first part of the speech contrasts with the aggravated, almost threatening, tone of the conclusion. He characteristically remarks that he will not speak as a rhetorician, that is to say, he will not make a regular defence such as Lysias or one of the orators might have composed for him, or, according to some accounts, did compose for him. But he first procures himself a hearing by conciliatory words. He does not attack the Sophists; for they were open to the same charges as himself; they were equally ridiculed by the Comic poets, and almost equally hateful to Anytus and Meletus. Yet incidentally the antagonism between Socrates and the Sophists is allowed to appear. He is poor and they are rich; his profession that he teaches nothing is opposed to their readiness to teach all things; his talking in the marketplace to their private instructions; his tarry-at-home life to their wandering from city to city. The tone which he assumes towards them is one of real friendliness, but also of concealed irony. Towards Anaxagoras, who had disappointed him in his hopes of learning about mind and nature, he shows a less kindly feeling, which is also the feeling of Plato in other passages (Laws). But Anaxagoras had been dead thirty years, and was beyond the reach of persecution.

It has been remarked that the prophecy of a new generation of teachers who would rebuke and exhort the Athenian people in harsher and more violent terms was, as far as we know, never fulfilled. No inference can be drawn from this circumstance as to the probability of the words attributed to him having been actually uttered. They express the aspiration of the first martyr of philosophy, that he would leave behind him many followers, accompanied by the not unnatural feeling that they would be fiercer and more inconsiderate in their words when emancipated from his control.

The above remarks must be understood as applying with any degree of certainty to the Platonic Socrates only. For, although these or similar words may have been spoken by Socrates himself, we cannot exclude the possibility, that like so much else, e.g. the wisdom of Critias, the poem of Solon, the virtues of Charmides, they may have been due only to the imagination of Plato. The arguments of those who maintain that the Apology was composed during the process, resting on no evidence, do not require a serious refutation. Nor are the reasonings of Schleiermacher, who argues that the Platonic defence is an exact or nearly exact reproduction of the words of Socrates, partly because Plato would not have been guilty of the impiety of altering them, and also because many points of the defence might have been improved and strengthened, at all more conclusive. (See English Translation.) What effect the death of Socrates produced on the mind of Plato, we cannot certainly determine; nor can we say how he would or must have written under the circumstances. We observe that the enmity of Aristophanes to Socrates does not prevent Plato from introducing them together in the Symposium engaged in friendly intercourse. Nor is there any trace in the Dialogues of an attempt to make Anytus or Meletus personally odious in the eyes of the Athenian public.

APOLOGY by Plato
Translated by Benjamin Jowett

How you, O Athenians, have been affected by my accusers, I cannot tell; but I know that they almost made me forget who I was--so persuasively did they speak; and yet they have hardly uttered a word of truth. But of the many falsehoods told by them, there was one which quite amazed me;--I mean when they said that you should be upon your guard and not allow yourselves to be deceived by the force of my eloquence. To say this, when they were certain to be detected as soon as I opened my lips and proved myself to be anything but a great speaker, did indeed appear to me most shameless--unless by the force of eloquence they mean the force of truth; for is such is their meaning, I admit that I am eloquent. But in how different a way from theirs! Well, as I was saying, they have scarcely spoken the truth at all; but from me you shall hear the whole truth: not, however, delivered after their manner in a set oration duly ornamented with words and phrases. No, by heaven! but I shall use the words and arguments which occur to me at the moment; for I am confident in the justice of my cause (Or, I am certain that I am right in taking this course.): at my time of life I ought not to be appearing before you, O men of Athens, in the character of a juvenile orator--let no one expect it of me. And I must beg of you to grant me a favour:--If I defend myself in my accustomed manner, and you hear me using the words which I have been in the habit of using in the agora, at the tables of the money-changers, or anywhere else, I would ask you not to be surprised, and not to interrupt me on this account. For I am more than seventy years of age, and appearing now for the first time in a court of law, I am quite a stranger to the language of the place; and therefore I would have you regard me as if I were really a stranger, whom you would excuse if he spoke in his native tongue, and after the fashion of his country:--Am I making an unfair request of you? Never mind the manner, which may or may not be good; but think only of the truth of my words, and give heed to that: let the speaker speak truly and the judge decide justly.

And first, I have to reply to the older charges and to my first accusers, and then I will go on to the later ones. For of old I have had many accusers, who have accused me falsely to you during many years; and I am more afraid of them than of Anytus and his associates, who are dangerous, too, in their own way. But far more dangerous are the others, who began when you were children, and took possession of your minds with their falsehoods, telling of one Socrates, a wise man, who speculated about the heaven above, and searched into the earth beneath, and made the worse appear the better cause. The disseminators of this tale are the accusers whom I dread; for their hearers are apt to fancy that such enquirers do not believe in the existence of the gods. And they are many, and their charges against me are of ancient date, and they were made by them in the days when you were more impressible than you are now--in childhood, or it may have been in youth--and the cause when heard went by default, for there was none to answer. And hardest of all, I do not know and cannot tell the names of my accusers; unless in the chance case of a Comic poet. All who from envy and malice have persuaded you--some of them having first convinced themselves--all this class of men are most difficult to deal with; for I cannot have them up here, and cross-examine them, and therefore I must simply fight with shadows in my own defence, and argue when there is no one who answers. I will ask you then to assume with me, as I was saying, that my opponents are of two kinds; one recent, the other ancient: and I hope that you will see the propriety of my answering the latter first, for these accusations you heard long before the others, and much oftener.

Well, then, I must make my defence, and endeavour to clear away in a short time, a slander which has lasted a long time. May I succeed, if to succeed be for my good and yours, or likely to avail me in my cause! The task is not an easy one; I quite understand the nature of it. And so leaving the event with God, in obedience to the law I will now make my defence.

I will begin at the beginning, and ask what is the accusation which has given rise to the slander of me, and in fact has encouraged Meletus to proof this charge against me. Well, what do the slanderers say? They shall be my prosecutors, and

I will sum up their words in an affidavit: 'Socrates is an evil-doer, and a curious person, who searches into things under the earth and in heaven, and he makes the worse appear the better cause; and he teaches the aforesaid doctrines to others.' Such is the nature of the accusation: it is just what you have yourselves seen in the comedy of Aristophanes (Aristoph., Clouds.), who has introduced a man whom he calls Socrates, going about and saying that he walks in air, and talking a deal of nonsense concerning matters of which I do not pretend to know either much or little--not that I mean to speak disparagingly of any one who is a student of natural philosophy. I should be very sorry if Meletus could bring so grave a charge against me. But the simple truth is, O Athenians, that I have nothing to do with physical speculations. Very many of those here present are witnesses to the truth of this, and to them I appeal. Speak then, you who have heard me, and tell your neighbours whether any of you have ever known me hold forth in few words or in many upon such matters...You hear their answer. And from what they say of this part of the charge you will be able to judge of the truth of the rest.

As little foundation is there for the report that I am a teacher, and take money; this accusation has no more truth in it than the other. Although, if a man were really able to instruct mankind, to receive money for giving instruction would, in my opinion, be an honour to him. There is Gorgias of Leontium, and Prodicus of Ceos, and Hippias of Elis, who go the round of the cities, and are able to persuade the young men to leave their own citizens by whom they might be taught for nothing, and come to them whom they not only pay, but are thankful if they may be allowed to pay them. There is at this time a Parian philosopher residing in Athens, of whom I have heard; and I came to hear of him in this way:--I came across a man who has spent a world of money on the Sophists, Callias, the son of Hipponicus, and knowing that he had sons, I asked him: 'Callias,' I said, 'if your two sons were foals or calves, there would be no difficulty in finding some one to put over them; we should hire a trainer of horses, or a farmer probably, who would improve and perfect them in their own proper virtue and excellence; but as they are human beings, whom are you thinking of placing over them? Is there any one who understands human and political virtue? You must have thought about the matter, for you have sons; is there any one?' 'There is,' he said. 'Who is he?' said I; 'and of what country? and what does he charge?' 'Evenus the Parian,' he replied; 'he is the man, and his charge is five minae.' Happy is Evenus, I said to myself, if he really has this wisdom, and teaches at such a moderate charge. Had I the same, I should have been very proud and conceited; but the truth is that I have no knowledge of the kind.

I dare say, Athenians, that some one among you will reply, 'Yes, Socrates, but what is the origin of these accusations which are brought against you; there must have been something strange which you have been doing? All these rumours and this talk about you would never have arisen if you had been like other men: tell us, then, what is the cause of them, for we should be sorry to judge hastily of you.' Now I regard this as a fair challenge, and I will endeavour to explain to you the reason why I am called wise and have such an evil fame. Please to attend then. And although some of you may think that I am joking, I declare that I will tell you the entire truth. Men of Athens, this reputation of mine has come of a certain sort of wisdom which I possess. If you ask me what kind of wisdom, I reply, wisdom such as may perhaps be attained by man, for to that extent I am inclined to believe that I am wise; whereas the persons of whom I was speaking have a superhuman wisdom which I may fail to describe, because I have it not myself; and he who says that I have, speaks falsely, and is taking away my character. And here, O men of Athens, I must beg you not to interrupt me, even if I seem to say something extravagant. For the word which I will speak is not mine. I will refer you to a witness who is worthy of credit; that witness shall be the God of Delphi--he will tell you about my wisdom, if I have any, and of what sort it is. You must have known Chaerephon; he was early a friend of mine, and also a friend of yours, for he shared in the recent exile of the people, and returned with you. Well, Chaerephon, as you know, was very impetuous in all his doings, and he went to Delphi and boldly asked the oracle to tell him whether--as I was saying, I must beg you not to interrupt--he asked the oracle to tell him whether anyone was wiser than I was, and the Pythian prophetess answered, that there was no man wiser. Chaerephon is dead himself; but his brother, who is in court, will confirm the truth of what I am saying.

Why do I mention this? Because I am going to explain to you why I have such an evil name. When I heard the answer, I said to myself, What can the god mean? and what is the interpretation of his riddle? for I know that I have no wisdom, small or great. What then can he mean when he says that I am the wisest of men? And yet he is a god, and cannot lie; that would be against his nature. After long consideration, I thought of a method of trying the question. I reflected that if I could only find a man wiser than myself, then I might go to the god with a refutation in my hand. I should say to him, 'Here is a man who is wiser than I am; but you said that I was the wisest.' Accordingly I went to one who had the reputation of wisdom, and observed him--his name I need not mention; he was a politician whom I selected for examination--and the result was as follows: When I began to talk with him, I could not help thinking that he was not really wise, although he was thought wise by many, and still wiser by himself; and thereupon I tried to explain to him that he thought himself wise, but was not really wise; and the consequence was that he hated me, and his enmity was shared by several who were present and heard me. So I left him, saying to myself, as I went away: Well, although I do not suppose that either of us knows anything really beautiful and good, I am better off than he is,-- for he knows nothing, and thinks that he knows; I neither know nor think that I know. In this latter particular, then, I seem to have slightly the advantage of him. Then I went to another who had still higher pretensions to wisdom, and my conclusion was exactly the same. Whereupon I made another enemy of him, and of many others besides him.

Then I went to one man after another, being not unconscious of the enmity which I provoked, and I lamented and feared this: but necessity was laid upon me,--the word of God, I thought, ought to be considered first. And I said to myself, Go I must to all who appear to know, and find out the meaning of the oracle. And I swear to you, Athenians, by the dog I swear! --for I must tell you the truth--the result of my mission was just this: I found that the men most in repute were all but the most foolish; and that others less esteemed were really wiser and better. I will tell you the tale of my wanderings and of the 'Herculean' labours, as I may call them, which I endured only to find at last the oracle irrefutable. After the politicians, I went to the poets; tragic, dithyrambic, and all sorts. And there, I said to myself, you will be instantly detected; now you will find out that you are more ignorant than they are. Accordingly, I took them some of the most elaborate passages in their own writings, and asked what was the meaning of them--thinking that they would teach me something. Will you believe me? I am almost ashamed to confess the truth, but I must say that there is hardly a person present who would not have talked better about their poetry than they did themselves. Then I knew that not by wisdom do poets write poetry, but by a sort of genius and inspiration; they are like diviners or soothsayers who also say many fine things, but do not understand the meaning of them. The poets appeared to me to be much in the same case; and I further observed that upon the strength of their poetry they believed themselves to be the wisest of men in other things in which they were not wise. So I departed, conceiving myself to be superior to them for the same reason that I was superior to the politicians.

At last I went to the artisans. I was conscious that I knew nothing at all, as I may say, and I was sure that they knew many fine things; and here I was not mistaken, for they did know many things of which I was ignorant, and in this they certainly were wiser than I was. But I observed that even the good artisans fell into the same error as the poets;--because they were good workmen they thought that they also knew all sorts of high matters, and this defect in them overshadowed their wisdom; and therefore I asked myself on behalf of the oracle, whether I would like to be as I was, neither having their knowledge nor their ignorance, or like them in both; and I made answer to myself and to the oracle that I was better off as I was.

This inquisition has led to my having many enemies of the worst and most dangerous kind, and has given occasion also to many calumnies. And I am called wise, for my hearers always imagine that I myself possess the wisdom which I find wanting in others: but the truth is, O men of Athens, that God only is wise; and by his answer he intends to show that the wisdom of men is worth little or nothing; he is not speaking of Socrates, he is only using my name by way of illustration, as if he said, He, O men, is the wisest, who, like Socrates, knows that his wisdom is in truth worth nothing. And so I go about the world, obedient to the god, and search and make enquiry into the wisdom of any one, whether citizen or stranger, who appears to be wise; and if he is not wise, then in vindication of the oracle I show him that he is not wise; and my occupation quite absorbs me, and I have no time to give either to any public matter of interest or to any concern of my own, but I am in utter poverty by reason of my devotion to the god.

There is another thing:--young men of the richer classes, who have not much to do, come about me of their own accord; they like to hear the pretenders examined, and they often imitate me, and proceed to examine others; there are plenty of persons, as they quickly discover, who think that they know something, but really know little or nothing; and then those who are examined by them instead of being angry with themselves are angry with me: This confounded Socrates, they say; this villainous misleader of youth!-- and then if somebody asks them, Why, what evil does he practise or teach? they do not know, and cannot tell; but in order that they may not appear to be at a loss, they repeat the ready-made charges which are used against all philosophers about teaching things up in the clouds and under the earth, and having no gods, and making the worse appear the better cause; for they do not like to confess that their pretence of knowledge has been detected-- which is the truth; and as they are numerous and ambitious and energetic, and are drawn up in battle array and have persuasive tongues, they have filled your ears with their loud and inveterate calumnies. And this is the reason why my three accusers, Meletus and Anytus and Lycon, have set upon me; Meletus, who has a quarrel with me on behalf of the poets; Anytus, on behalf of the craftsmen and politicians; Lycon, on behalf of the rhetoricians: and as I said at the beginning, I cannot expect to get rid of such a mass of calumny all in a moment. And this, O men of Athens, is the truth and the whole truth; I have concealed nothing, I have dissembled nothing. And yet, I know that my plainness of speech makes them hate me, and what is their hatred but a proof that I am speaking the truth?--Hence has arisen the prejudice against me; and this is the reason of it, as you will find out either in this or in any future enquiry.

I have said enough in my defence against the first class of my accusers; I turn to the second class. They are headed by Meletus, that good man and true lover of his country, as he calls himself. Against these, too, I must try to make a defence:-- Let their affidavit be read: it contains something of this kind: It says that Socrates is a doer of evil, who corrupts the youth; and who does not believe in the gods of the state, but has other new divinities of his own. Such is the charge; and now let us examine the particular counts. He says that I am a doer of evil, and corrupt the youth; but I say, O men of Athens, that Meletus is a doer of evil, in that he pretends to be in earnest when he is only in jest, and is so eager to bring men to trial from a pretended zeal and interest about matters in which he really never had the smallest interest. And the truth of this I will endeavour to prove to you.

Come hither, Meletus, and let me ask a question of you. You think a great deal about the improvement of youth?

Yes, I do.

Tell the judges, then, who is their improver; for you must know, as you have taken the pains to discover their corrupter, and are citing and accusing me before them. Speak, then, and tell the judges who their improver is.--Observe, Meletus, that you are silent, and have nothing to say. But is not this rather disgraceful, and a very considerable proof of what I was saying, that you have no interest in the matter? Speak up, friend, and tell us who their improver is.

The laws.

But that, my good sir, is not my meaning. I want to know who the person is, who, in the first place, knows the laws.

The judges, Socrates, who are present in court.

What, do you mean to say, Meletus, that they are able to instruct and improve youth?

Certainly they are.

What, all of them, or some only and not others?

All of them.

By the goddess Here, that is good news! There are plenty of improvers, then. And what do you say of the audience,--do they improve them?

Yes, they do.

And the senators?

Yes, the senators improve them.

But perhaps the members of the assembly corrupt them?--or do they too improve them?

They improve them.

Then every Athenian improves and elevates them; all with the exception of myself; and I alone am their corrupter? Is that what you affirm?

That is what I stoutly affirm.

I am very unfortunate if you are right. But suppose I ask you a question: How about horses? Does one man do them harm and all the world good? Is not the exact opposite the truth? One man is able to do them good, or at least not many;--the trainer of horses, that is to say, does them good, and others who have to do with them rather injure them? Is not that true, Meletus, of horses, or of any other animals? Most assuredly it is; whether you and Anytus say yes or no. Happy indeed would be the condition of youth if they had one corrupter only, and all the rest of the world were their improvers. But you, Meletus, have sufficiently shown that you never had a thought about the young: your carelessness is seen in your not caring about the very things which you bring against me.

And now, Meletus, I will ask you another question--by Zeus I will: Which is better, to live among bad citizens, or among good ones? Answer, friend, I say; the question is one which may be easily answered. Do not the good do their neighbours good, and the bad do them evil?

Certainly.

And is there anyone who would rather be injured than benefited by those who live with him? Answer, my good friend, the law requires you to answer-- does any one like to be injured?

Certainly not.

And when you accuse me of corrupting and deteriorating the youth, do you allege that I corrupt them intentionally or unintentionally?

Intentionally, I say.

But you have just admitted that the good do their neighbours good, and the evil do them evil. Now, is that a truth which your superior wisdom has recognized thus early in life, and am I, at my age, in such darkness and ignorance as not to know that if a man with whom I have to live is corrupted by me, I am very likely to be harmed by him; and yet I corrupt him, and intentionally, too--so you say, although neither I nor any other human being is ever likely to be convinced by you. But either I do not corrupt them, or I corrupt them unintentionally; and on either view of the case you lie. If my offence is unintentional, the law has no cognizance of unintentional offences: you ought to have taken me privately, and warned and admonished me; for if I had been better advised, I should have left off doing what I only did unintentionally--no doubt I should; but you would have nothing to say to me and refused to teach me. And now you bring me up in this court, which is a place not of instruction, but of punishment.

It will be very clear to you, Athenians, as I was saying, that Meletus has no care at all, great or small, about the matter. But still I should like to know, Meletus, in what I am affirmed to corrupt the young. I suppose you mean, as I infer from your indictment, that I teach them not to acknowledge the gods which the state acknowledges, but some other new divinities or spiritual agencies in their stead. These are the lessons by which I corrupt the youth, as you say.

Yes, that I say emphatically.

Then, by the gods, Meletus, of whom we are speaking, tell me and the court, in somewhat plainer terms, what you mean! for I do not as yet understand whether you affirm that I teach other men to acknowledge some gods, and therefore that I do believe in gods, and am not an entire atheist--this you do not lay to my charge,--but only you say that they are not the same gods which the city recognizes--the charge is that they are different gods. Or, do you mean that I am an atheist simply, and a teacher of atheism?

I mean the latter--that you are a complete atheist.

What an extraordinary statement! Why do you think so, Meletus? Do you mean that I do not believe in the godhead of the sun or moon, like other men?

I assure you, judges, that he does not: for he says that the sun is stone, and the moon earth.

Friend Meletus, you think that you are accusing Anaxagoras: and you have but a bad opinion of the judges, if you fancy them illiterate to such a degree as not to know that these doctrines are found in the books of Anaxagoras the Clazomenian, which are full of them. And so, forsooth, the youth are said to be taught them by Socrates, when there are not unfrequently exhibitions of them at the theatre (Probably in allusion to Aristophanes who caricatured, and to Euripides who borrowed the notions of Anaxagoras, as well as to other dramatic poets.) (price of admission one drachma at the most); and they might pay their money, and laugh at Socrates if he pretends to father these extraordinary views. And so, Meletus, you really think that I do not believe in any god?

I swear by Zeus that you believe absolutely in none at all.

Nobody will believe you, Meletus, and I am pretty sure that you do not believe yourself. I cannot help thinking, men of Athens, that Meletus is reckless and impudent, and that he has written this indictment in a spirit of mere wantonness and youthful bravado. Has he not compounded a riddle, thinking to try me? He said to himself:--I shall see whether the wise Socrates will discover my facetious contradiction, or whether I shall be able to deceive him and the rest of them. For he certainly does appear to me to contradict himself in the indictment as much as if he said that Socrates is guilty of not believing in the gods, and yet of believing in them--but this is not like a person who is in earnest.

I should like you, O men of Athens, to join me in examining what I conceive to be his inconsistency; and do you, Meletus, answer. And I must remind the audience of my request that they would not make a disturbance if I speak in my accustomed manner:

Did ever man, Meletus, believe in the existence of human things, and not of human beings?...I wish, men of Athens, that he would answer, and not be always trying to get up an interruption. Did ever any man believe in horsemanship, and not in horses? or in flute-playing, and not in flute- players? No, my friend; I will answer to you and to the court, as you refuse to answer for yourself. There is no man who ever did. But now please to answer the next question: Can a man believe in spiritual and divine agencies, and not in spirits or demigods?

He cannot.

How lucky I am to have extracted that answer, by the assistance of the court! But then you swear in the indictment that I teach and believe in divine or spiritual agencies (new or old, no matter for that); at any rate, I believe in spiritual agencies,--so you say and swear in the affidavit; and yet if I believe in divine beings, how can I help believing in spirits or demigods;--must I not? To be sure I must; and therefore I may assume that your silence gives consent. Now what are spirits or demigods? Are they not either gods or the sons of gods?

Certainly they are.

But this is what I call the facetious riddle invented by you: the demigods or spirits are gods, and you say first that I do not believe in gods, and then again that I do believe in gods; that is, if I believe in demigods. For if the demigods are the illegitimate sons of gods, whether by the nymphs or by any other mothers, of whom they are said to be the sons--what human being will ever believe that there are no gods if they are the sons of gods? You might as well affirm the existence of mules, and deny that of horses and asses. Such nonsense, Meletus, could only have been intended by you to make trial of me. You have put this into the indictment because you had nothing real of which to accuse me. But no one who has a particle of understanding will ever be convinced by you that the same men can believe in divine and superhuman things, and yet not believe that there are gods and demigods and heroes.

I have said enough in answer to the charge of Meletus: any elaborate defence is unnecessary, but I know only too well how many are the enmities which I have incurred, and this is what will be my destruction if I am destroyed;--not Meletus, nor yet Anytus, but the envy and detraction of the world, which has been the death of many good men, and will probably be the death of many more; there is no danger of my being the last of them.

Some one will say: And are you not ashamed, Socrates, of a course of life which is likely to bring you to an untimely end? To him I may fairly answer: There you are mistaken: a man who is good for anything ought not to calculate the chance of living or dying; he ought only to consider whether in doing anything he is doing right or wrong--acting the part of a good man or of a bad. Whereas, upon your view, the heroes who fell at Troy were not good for much, and the son of Thetis above all, who altogether despised danger in comparison with disgrace; and when he was so eager to slay Hector, his goddess mother said to him, that if he avenged his companion Patroclus, and slew Hector, he would die himself--'Fate,' she said, in these or the like words, 'waits for you next after Hector;' he, receiving this warning, utterly despised danger and death, and instead of fearing them, feared rather to live in dishonour, and not to avenge his friend. 'Let me die forthwith,' he replies, 'and be avenged of my enemy, rather than abide here by the beaked ships, a laughing-stock and a burden of the earth.' Had Achilles any thought of death and danger? For wherever a man's place is, whether the place which he has chosen or that in which he has been placed by a commander, there he ought to remain in the hour of danger; he should not think of death or of anything but of disgrace. And this, O men of Athens, is a true saying.

Strange, indeed, would be my conduct, O men of Athens, if I who, when I was ordered by the generals whom you chose to command me at Potidaea and Amphipolis and Delium, remained where they placed me, like any other man, facing death--if now, when, as I conceive and imagine, God orders me to fulfil the philosopher's mission of searching into myself and other men, I were to desert my post through fear of death, or any other fear; that would indeed be strange, and I might justly be arraigned in court for denying the existence of the gods, if I disobeyed the oracle because I was afraid of death, fancying that I was wise when I was not wise.

For the fear of death is indeed the pretence of wisdom, and not real wisdom, being a pretence of knowing the unknown; and no one knows whether death, which men in their fear apprehend to be the greatest evil, may not be the greatest good. Is not this ignorance of a disgraceful sort, the ignorance which is the conceit that a man knows what he does not know? And in this respect only I believe myself to differ from men in general, and may perhaps claim to be wiser than they are:--that whereas I know but little of the world below, I do not suppose that I know: but I do know that injustice and disobedience to a better, whether God or man, is evil and dishonourable, and I will never fear or avoid a possible good rather than a certain evil. And therefore if you let me go now, and are not convinced by Anytus, who said that since I had been prosecuted I must be put to death; (or if not that I ought never to have been prosecuted at all); and that if I escape now, your sons will all be utterly ruined by listening to my words--if you say to me, Socrates, this time we will not mind Anytus, and you shall be let off, but upon one condition, that you are not to enquire and speculate in this way any more, and that if you are caught doing so again you shall die;--if this was the condition on which you let me go, I should reply: Men of Athens, I honour and love you; but I shall obey God rather than you, and while I have life and strength I shall never cease from the practice and teaching of philosophy, exhorting any one whom I meet and saying to him after my manner: You, my friend,--a citizen of the great and mighty and wise city of Athens,--are you not ashamed of heaping up the greatest amount of money and honour and reputation, and caring so little about wisdom and truth and the greatest improvement of the soul, which you never regard or heed at all? And if the person with whom I am arguing, says: Yes, but I do care; then I do not leave him or let him go at once; but I proceed to interrogate and examine and cross-examine him, and if I think that he has no virtue in him, but only says that he has, I reproach him with undervaluing the greater, and overvaluing the less. And I shall repeat the same words to every one whom I meet, young and old, citizen and alien, but especially to the citizens, inasmuch as they are my brethren. For know that this is the command of God; and I believe that no greater good has ever happened in the state than my service to the God. For I do nothing but go about persuading you all, old and young alike, not to take thought for your persons or your properties, but first and chiefly to care about the greatest improvement of the soul. I tell you that virtue is not given by money, but that from virtue comes money and every other good of man, public as well as private. This is my teaching, and if this is the doctrine which corrupts the youth, I am a mischievous person. But if any one says that this is not my teaching, he is speaking an untruth. Wherefore, O men of Athens, I say to you, do as Anytus bids or not as Anytus bids, and either acquit me or not; but whichever you do, understand that I shall never alter my ways, not even if I have to die many times.

Men of Athens, do not interrupt, but hear me; there was an understanding between us that you should hear me to the end: I have something more to say, at which you may be inclined to cry out; but I believe that to hear me will be good for you, and therefore I beg that you will not cry out. I would have you know, that if you kill such an one as I am, you will injure yourselves more than you will injure me. Nothing will injure me, not Meletus nor yet Anytus--they cannot, for a bad man is not permitted to injure a better than himself. I do not deny that Anytus may, perhaps, kill him, or drive him into exile, or deprive him of civil rights; and he may imagine, and others may imagine, that he is inflicting a great injury upon him: but there I do not agree. For the evil of doing as he is doing--the evil of unjustly taking away the life of another--is greater far.

And now, Athenians, I am not going to argue for my own sake, as you may think, but for yours, that you may not sin against the God by condemning me, who am his gift to you. For if you kill me you will not easily find a successor to me, who, if I may use such a ludicrous figure of speech, am a sort of gadfly, given to the state by God; and the state is a great and noble steed who is tardy in his motions owing to his very size, and requires to be stirred into life. I am that gadfly which God has attached to the state, and all day long and in all places am always fastening upon you, arousing and persuading and reproaching you. You will not easily find another like me, and therefore I would advise you to spare me. I dare say that you may feel out of temper (like a person who is suddenly awakened from sleep), and you think that you might easily strike me dead as Anytus advises, and then you would sleep on for the remainder of your lives, unless God in his care of you sent you another gadfly. When I say that I am given to you by God, the proof of my mission is this:--if I had been like other men, I should not have neglected all my own concerns or patiently seen the neglect of them during all these years, and have been doing yours, coming to you individually like a father or elder brother, exhorting you to regard virtue;

such conduct, I say, would be unlike human nature. If I had gained anything, or if my exhortations had been paid, there would have been some sense in my doing so; but now, as you will perceive, not even the impudence of my accusers dares to say that I have ever exacted or sought pay of any one; of that they have no witness. And I have a sufficient witness to the truth of what I say--my poverty.

Some one may wonder why I go about in private giving advice and busying myself with the concerns of others, but do not venture to come forward in public and advise the state. I will tell you why. You have heard me speak at sundry times and in divers places of an oracle or sign which comes to me, and is the divinity which Meletus ridicules in the indictment. This sign, which is a kind of voice, first began to come to me when I was a child; it always forbids but never commands me to do anything which I am going to do. This is what deters me from being a politician. And rightly, as I think. For I am certain, O men of Athens, that if I had engaged in politics, I should have perished long ago, and done no good either to you or to myself. And do not be offended at my telling you the truth: for the truth is, that no man who goes to war with you or any other multitude, honestly striving against the many lawless and unrighteous deeds which are done in a state, will save his life; he who will fight for the right, if he would live even for a brief space, must have a private station and not a public one.

I can give you convincing evidence of what I say, not words only, but what you value far more--actions. Let me relate to you a passage of my own life which will prove to you that I should never have yielded to injustice from any fear of death, and that 'as I should have refused to yield' I must have died at once. I will tell you a tale of the courts, not very interesting perhaps, but nevertheless true. The only office of state which I ever held, O men of Athens, was that of senator: the tribe Antiochis, which is my tribe, had the presidency at the trial of the generals who had not taken up the bodies of the slain after the battle of Arginusae; and you proposed to try them in a body, contrary to law, as you all thought afterwards; but at the time I was the only one of the Prytanes who was opposed to the illegality, and I gave my vote against you; and when the orators threatened to impeach and arrest me, and you called and shouted, I made up my mind that I would run the risk, having law and justice with me, rather than take part in your injustice because I feared imprisonment and death. This happened in the days of the democracy. But when the oligarchy of the Thirty was in power, they sent for me and four others into the rotunda, and bade us bring Leon the Salaminian from Salamis, as they wanted to put him to death. This was a specimen of the sort of commands which they were always giving with the view of implicating as many as possible in their crimes; and then I showed, not in word only but in deed, that, if I may be allowed to use such an expression, I cared not a straw for death, and that my great and only care was lest I should do an unrighteous or unholy thing. For the strong arm of that oppressive power did not frighten me into doing wrong; and when we came out of the rotunda the other four went to Salamis and fetched Leon, but I went quietly home. For which I might have lost my life, had not the power of the Thirty shortly afterwards come to an end. And many will witness to my words.

Now do you really imagine that I could have survived all these years, if I had led a public life, supposing that like a good man I had always maintained the right and had made justice, as I ought, the first thing? No indeed, men of Athens, neither I nor any other man. But I have been always the same in all my actions, public as well as private, and never have I yielded any base compliance to those who are slanderously termed my disciples, or to any other. Not that I have any regular disciples. But if any one likes to come and hear me while I am pursuing my mission, whether he be young or old, he is not excluded. Nor do I converse only with those who pay; but any one, whether he be rich or poor, may ask and answer me and listen to my words; and whether he turns out to be a bad man or a good one, neither result can be justly imputed to me; for I never taught or professed to teach him anything. And if any one says that he has ever learned or heard anything from me in private which all the world has not heard, let me tell you that he is lying.

But I shall be asked, Why do people delight in continually conversing with you? I have told you already, Athenians, the whole truth about this matter: they like to hear the cross-examination of the pretenders to wisdom; there is amusement in it. Now this duty of cross-examining other men has been imposed upon me by God; and has been signified to me by oracles, visions, and in every way in which the will of divine power was ever intimated to any one. This is true, O Athenians, or, if not true, would be soon refuted. If I am or have been corrupting the youth, those of them who are now grown up and have become sensible that I gave them bad advice in the days of their youth should come forward as accusers, and take their revenge;

or if they do not like to come themselves, some of their relatives, fathers, brothers, or other kinsmen, should say what evil their families have suffered at my hands. Now is their time. Many of them I see in the court. There is Crito, who is of the same age and of the same deme with myself, and there is Critobulus his son, whom I also see. Then again there is Lysanias of Sphettus, who is the father of Aeschines--he is present; and also there is Antiphon of Cephisus, who is the father of Epigenes; and there are the brothers of several who have associated with me. There is Nicostratus the son of Theosdotides, and the brother of Theodotus (now Theodotus himself is dead, and therefore he, at any rate, will not seek to stop him); and there is Paralus the son of Demodocus, who had a brother Theages; and Adeimantus the son of Ariston, whose brother Plato is present; and Aeantodorus, who is the brother of Apollodorus, whom I also see. I might mention a great many others, some of whom Meletus should have produced as witnesses in the course of his speech; and let him still produce them, if he has forgotten--I will make way for him. And let him say, if he has any testimony of the sort which he can produce. Nay, Athenians, the very opposite is the truth. For all these are ready to witness on behalf of the corrupter, of the injurer of their kindred, as Meletus and Anytus call me; not the corrupted youth only--there might have been a motive for that--but their uncorrupted elder relatives. Why should they too support me with their testimony? Why, indeed, except for the sake of truth and justice, and because they know that I am speaking the truth, and that Meletus is a liar.

Well, Athenians, this and the like of this is all the defence which I have to offer. Yet a word more. Perhaps there may be some one who is offended at me, when he calls to mind how he himself on a similar, or even a less serious occasion, prayed and entreated the judges with many tears, and how he produced his children in court, which was a moving spectacle, together with a host of relations and friends; whereas I, who am probably in danger of my life, will do none of these things. The contrast may occur to his mind, and he may be set against me, and vote in anger because he is displeased at me on this account. Now if there be such a person among you,--mind, I do not say that there is,--to him I may fairly reply: My friend, I am a man, and like other men, a creature of flesh and blood, and not 'of wood or stone,' as Homer says; and I have a family, yes, and sons, O Athenians, three in number, one almost a man, and two others who are still young; and yet I will not bring any of them hither in order to petition you for an acquittal. And why not? Not from any self-assertion or want of respect for you. Whether I am or am not afraid of death is another question, of which I will not now speak. But, having regard to public opinion, I feel that such conduct would be discreditable to myself, and to you, and to the whole state. One who has reached my years, and who has a name for wisdom, ought not to demean himself. Whether this opinion of me be deserved or not, at any rate the world has decided that Socrates is in some way superior to other men. And if those among you who are said to be superior in wisdom and courage, and any other virtue, demean themselves in this way, how shameful is their conduct! I have seen men of reputation, when they have been condemned, behaving in the strangest manner: they seemed to fancy that they were going to suffer something dreadful if they died, and that they could be immortal if you only allowed them to live; and I think that such are a dishonour to the state, and that any stranger coming in would have said of them that the most eminent men of Athens, to whom the Athenians themselves give honour and command, are no better than women. And I say that these things ought not to be done by those of us who have a reputation; and if they are done, you ought not to permit them; you ought rather to show that you are far more disposed to condemn the man who gets up a doleful scene and makes the city ridiculous, than him who holds his peace.

But, setting aside the question of public opinion, there seems to be something wrong in asking a favour of a judge, and thus procuring an acquittal, instead of informing and convincing him. For his duty is, not to make a present of justice, but to give judgment; and he has sworn that he will judge according to the laws, and not according to his own good pleasure; and we ought not to encourage you, nor should you allow yourselves to be encouraged, in this habit of perjury--there can be no piety in that. Do not then require me to do what I consider dishonourable and impious and wrong, especially now, when I am being tried for impiety on the indictment of Meletus. For if, O men of Athens, by force of persuasion and entreaty I could overpower your oaths, then I should be teaching you to believe that there are no gods, and in defending should simply convict myself of the charge of not believing in them. But that is not so--far otherwise. For I do believe that there are gods, and in a sense higher than that in which any of my accusers believe in them. And to you and to God I commit my cause, to be determined by you as is best for you and me.

There are many reasons why I am not grieved, O men of Athens, at the vote of condemnation. I expected it, and am only surprised that the votes are so nearly equal; for I had thought that the majority against me would have been far larger; but now, had thirty votes gone over to the other side, I should have been acquitted. And I may say, I think, that I have escaped Meletus. I may say more; for without the assistance of Anytus and Lycon, any one may see that he would not have had a fifth part of the votes, as the law requires, in which case he would have incurred a fine of a thousand drachmae.

And so he proposes death as the penalty. And what shall I propose on my part, O men of Athens? Clearly that which is my due. And what is my due? What return shall be made to the man who has never had the wit to be idle during his whole life; but has been careless of what the many care for-- wealth, and family interests, and military offices, and speaking in the assembly, and magistracies, and plots, and parties. Reflecting that I was really too honest a man to be a politician and live, I did not go where I could do no good to you or to myself; but where I could do the greatest good privately to every one of you, thither I went, and sought to persuade every man among you that he must look to himself, and seek virtue and wisdom before he looks to his private interests, and look to the state before he looks to the interests of the state; and that this should be the order which he observes in all his actions. What shall be done to such an one? Doubtless some good thing, O men of Athens, if he has his reward; and the good should be of a kind suitable to him. What would be a reward suitable to a poor man who is your benefactor, and who desires leisure that he may instruct you? There can be no reward so fitting as maintenance in the Prytaneum, O men of Athens, a reward which he deserves far more than the citizen who has won the prize at Olympia in the horse or chariot race, whether the chariots were drawn by two horses or by many. For I am in want, and he has enough; and he only gives you the appearance of happiness, and I give you the reality. And if I am to estimate the penalty fairly, I should say that maintenance in the Prytaneum is the just return.

Perhaps you think that I am braving you in what I am saying now, as in what I said before about the tears and prayers. But this is not so. I speak rather because I am convinced that I never intentionally wronged any one, although I cannot convince you--the time has been too short; if there were a law at Athens, as there is in other cities, that a capital cause should not be decided in one day, then I believe that I should have convinced you. But I cannot in a moment refute great slanders; and, as I am convinced that I never wronged another, I will assuredly not wrong myself. I will not say of myself that I deserve any evil, or propose any penalty. Why should I? because I am afraid of the penalty of death which Meletus proposes? When I do not know whether death is a good or an evil, why should I propose a penalty which would certainly be an evil? Shall I say imprisonment? And why should I live in prison, and be the slave of the magistrates of the year--of the Eleven? Or shall the penalty be a fine, and imprisonment until the fine is paid? There is the same objection. I should have to lie in prison, for money I have none, and cannot pay. And if I say exile (and this may possibly be the penalty which you will affix), I must indeed be blinded by the love of life, if I am so irrational as to expect that when you, who are my own citizens, cannot endure my discourses and words, and have found them so grievous and odious that you will have no more of them, others are likely to endure me. No indeed, men of Athens, that is not very likely. And what a life should I lead, at my age, wandering from city to city, ever changing my place of exile, and always being driven out! For I am quite sure that wherever I go, there, as here, the young men will flock to me; and if I drive them away, their elders will drive me out at their request; and if I let them come, their fathers and friends will drive me out for their sakes.

Some one will say: Yes, Socrates, but cannot you hold your tongue, and then you may go into a foreign city, and no one will interfere with you? Now I have great difficulty in making you understand my answer to this. For if I tell you that to do as you say would be a disobedience to the God, and therefore that I cannot hold my tongue, you will not believe that I am serious; and if I say again that daily to discourse about virtue, and of those other things about which you hear me examining myself and others, is the greatest good of man, and that the unexamined life is not worth living, you are still less likely to believe me. Yet I say what is true, although a thing of which it is hard for me to persuade you. Also, I have never been accustomed to think that I deserve to suffer any harm. Had I money I might have estimated the offence at what I was able to pay, and not have been much the worse. But I have none, and therefore I must ask you to proportion the fine to my means. Well, perhaps I could afford a mina, and therefore I propose that penalty: Plato, Crito, Critobulus, and Apollodorus, my friends here, bid me say thirty minae, and they will be the sureties. Let thirty minae be the penalty; for which sum they will be ample security to you.

...

Not much time will be gained, O Athenians, in return for the evil name which you will get from the detractors of the city, who will say that you killed Socrates, a wise man; for they will call me wise, even although I am not wise, when they want to reproach you. If you had waited a little while, your desire would have been fulfilled in the course of nature. For I am far advanced in years, as you may perceive, and not far from death. I am speaking now not to all of you, but only to those who have condemned me to death. And I have another thing to say to them: you think that I was convicted because I had no words of the sort which would have procured my acquittal--I mean, if I had thought fit to leave nothing undone or unsaid. Not so; the deficiency which led to my conviction was not of words-- certainly not. But I had not the boldness or impudence or inclination to address you as you would have liked me to do, weeping and wailing and lamenting, and saying and doing many things which you have been accustomed to hear from others, and which, as I maintain, are unworthy of me. I thought at the time that I ought not to do anything common or mean when in danger: nor do I now repent of the style of my defence; I would rather die having spoken after my manner, than speak in your manner and live. For neither in war nor yet at law ought I or any man to use every way of escaping death. Often in battle there can be no doubt that if a man will throw away his arms, and fall on his knees before his pursuers, he may escape death; and in other dangers there are other ways of escaping death, if a man is willing to say and do anything. The difficulty, my friends, is not to avoid death, but to avoid unrighteousness; for that runs faster than death. I am old and move slowly, and the slower runner has overtaken me, and my accusers are keen and quick, and the faster runner, who is unrighteousness, has overtaken them. And now I depart hence condemned by you to suffer the penalty of death,--they too go their ways condemned by the truth to suffer the penalty of villainy and wrong; and I must abide by my award--let them abide by theirs. I suppose that these things may be regarded as fated,--and I think that they are well.

And now, O men who have condemned me, I would fain prophesy to you; for I am about to die, and in the hour of death men are gifted with prophetic power. And I prophesy to you who are my murderers, that immediately after my departure punishment far heavier than you have inflicted on me will surely await you. Me you have killed because you wanted to escape the accuser, and not to give an account of your lives. But that will not be as you suppose: far otherwise. For I say that there will be more accusers of you than there are now; accusers whom hitherto I have restrained: and as they are younger they will be more inconsiderate with you, and you will be more offended at them. If you think that by killing men you can prevent some one from censuring your evil lives, you are mistaken; that is not a way of escape which is either possible or honourable; the easiest and the noblest way is not to be disabling others, but to be improving yourselves. This is the prophecy which I utter before my departure to the judges who have condemned me.

Friends, who would have acquitted me, I would like also to talk with you about the thing which has come to pass, while the magistrates are busy, and before I go to the place at which I must die. Stay then a little, for we may as well talk with one another while there is time. You are my friends, and I should like to show you the meaning of this event which has happened to me. O my judges--for you I may truly call judges--I should like to tell you of a wonderful circumstance. Hitherto the divine faculty of which the internal oracle is the source has constantly been in the habit of opposing me even about trifles, if I was going to make a slip or error in any matter; and now as you see there has come upon me that which may be thought, and is generally believed to be, the last and worst evil. But the oracle made no sign of opposition, either when I was leaving my house in the morning, or when I was on my way to the court, or while I was speaking, at anything which I was going to say; and yet I have often been stopped in the middle of a speech, but now in nothing

I either said or did touching the matter in hand has the oracle opposed me. What do I take to be the explanation of this silence? I will tell you. It is an intimation that what has happened to me is a good, and that those of us who think that death is an evil are in error. For the customary sign would surely have opposed me had I been going to evil and not to good.

Let us reflect in another way, and we shall see that there is great reason to hope that death is a good; for one of two things--either death is a state of nothingness and utter unconsciousness, or, as men say, there is a change and migration of the soul from this world to another. Now if you suppose that there is no consciousness, but a sleep like the sleep of him who is undisturbed even by dreams, death will be an unspeakable gain. For if a person were to select the night in which his sleep was undisturbed even by dreams, and were to compare with this the other days and nights of his life, and then were to tell us how many days and nights he had passed in the course of his life better and more pleasantly than this one, I think that any man, I will not say a private man, but even the great king will not find many such days or nights, when compared with the others. Now if death be of such a nature, I say that to die is gain; for eternity is then only a single night. But if death is the journey to another place, and there, as men say, all the dead abide, what good, O my friends and judges, can be greater than this? If indeed when the pilgrim arrives in the world below, he is delivered from the professors of justice in this world, and finds the true judges who are said to give judgment there, Minos and Rhadamanthus and Aeacus and Triptolemus, and other sons of God who were righteous in their own life, that pilgrimage will be worth making. What would not a man give if he might converse with Orpheus and Musaeus and Hesiod and Homer? Nay, if this be true, let me die again and again. I myself, too, shall have a wonderful interest in there meeting and conversing with Palamedes, and Ajax the son of Telamon, and any other ancient hero who has suffered death through an unjust judgment; and there will be no small pleasure, as I think, in comparing my own sufferings with theirs. Above all, I shall then be able to continue my search into true and false knowledge; as in this world, so also in the next; and I shall find out who is wise, and who pretends to be wise, and is not. What would not a man give, O judges, to be able to examine the leader of the great Trojan expedition; or Odysseus or Sisyphus, or numberless others, men and women too! What infinite delight would there be in conversing with them and asking them questions! In another world they do not put a man to death for asking questions: assuredly not. For besides being happier than we are, they will be immortal, if what is said is true.

Wherefore, O judges, be of good cheer about death, and know of a certainty, that no evil can happen to a good man, either in life or after death. He and his are not neglected by the gods; nor has my own approaching end happened by mere chance. But I see clearly that the time had arrived when it was better for me to die and be released from trouble; wherefore the oracle gave no sign. For which reason, also, I am not angry with my condemners, or with my accusers; they have done me no harm, although they did not mean to do me any good; and for this I may gently blame them.

Still I have a favour to ask of them. When my sons are grown up, I would ask you, O my friends, to punish them; and I would have you trouble them, as I have troubled you, if they seem to care about riches, or anything, more than about virtue; or if they pretend to be something when they are really nothing,--then reprove them, as I have reproved you, for not caring about that for which they ought to care, and thinking that they are something when they are really nothing. And if you do this, both I and my sons will have received justice at your hands.

The hour of departure has arrived, and we go our ways--I to die, and you to live. Which is better God only knows.

www.bookjungle.com *email: sales@bookjungle.com fax: 630-214-0564 mail: Book Jungle PO Box 2226 Champaign, IL 61825*

The Codes Of Hammurabi And Moses
W. W. Davies

QTY

The discovery of the Hammurabi Code is one of the greatest achievements of archaeology, and is of paramount interest, not only to the student of the Bible, but also to all those interested in ancient history...

Religion **ISBN:** *1-59462-338-4* **Pages:** 132 *MSRP $12.95*

The Theory of Moral Sentiments
Adam Smith

QTY

This work from 1749. contains original theories of conscience amd moral judgment and it is the foundation for systemof morals.

Philosophy **ISBN:** *1-59462-777-0* **Pages:** 536 *MSRP $19.95*

Jessica's First Prayer
Hesba Stretton

QTY

In a screened and secluded corner of one of the many railway-bridges which span the streets of London there could be seen a few years ago, from five o'clock every morning until half past eight, a tidily set-out coffee-stall, consisting of a trestle and board, upon which stood two large tin cans, with a small fire of charcoal burning under each so as to keep the coffee boiling during the early hours of the morning when the work-people were thronging into the city on their way to their daily toil...

Childrens **ISBN:** *1-59462-373-2* **Pages:** 84 *MSRP $9.95*

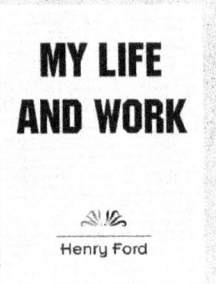

My Life and Work
Henry Ford

QTY

Henry Ford revolutionized the world with his implementation of mass production for the Model T automobile. Gain valuable business insight into his life and work with his own auto-biography... "We have only started on our development of our country we have not as yet, with all our talk of wonderful progress, done more than scratch the surface. The progress has been wonderful enough but..."

Biographies/ **ISBN:** *1-59462-198-5* **Pages:** 300 *MSRP $21.95*

www.bookjungle.com *email: sales@bookjungle.com fax: 630-214-0564 mail: Book Jungle PO Box 2226 Champaign, IL 61825*

The Art of Cross-Examination
Francis Wellman

QTY

I presume it is the experience of every author, after his first book is published upon an important subject, to be almost overwhelmed with a wealth of ideas and illustrations which could readily have been included in his book, and which to his own mind, at least, seem to make a second edition inevitable. Such certainly was the case with me; and when the first edition had reached its sixth impression in five months, I rejoiced to learn that it seemed to my publishers that the book had met with a sufficiently favorable reception to justify a second and considerably enlarged edition. ...

Reference   ISBN: *1-59462-647-2*   Pages:412   MSRP *$19.95*

On the Duty of Civil Disobedience
Henry David Thoreau

QTY

Thoreau wrote his famous essay, On the Duty of Civil Disobedience, as a protest against an unjust but popular war and the immoral but popular institution of slave-owning. He did more than write—he declined to pay his taxes, and was hauled off to gaol in consequence. Who can say how much this refusal of his hastened the end of the war and of slavery?

Law   ISBN: *1-59462-747-9*   Pages:48   MSRP *$7.45*

Dream Psychology Psychoanalysis for Beginners
Sigmund Freud

QTY

Sigmund Freud, born Sigismund Schlomo Freud (May 6, 1856 - September 23, 1939), was a Jewish-Austrian neurologist and psychiatrist who co-founded the psychoanalytic school of psychology. Freud is best known for his theories of the unconscious mind, especially involving the mechanism of repression; his redefinition of sexual desire as mobile and directed towards a wide variety of objects; and his therapeutic techniques, especially his understanding of transference in the therapeutic relationship and the presumed value of dreams as sources of insight into unconscious desires.

Psychology   ISBN: *1-59462-905-6*   Pages:196   MSRP *$15.45*

The Miracle of Right Thought
Orison Swett Marden

QTY

Believe with all of your heart that you will do what you were made to do. When the mind has once formed the habit of holding cheerful, happy, prosperous pictures, it will not be easy to form the opposite habit. It does not matter how improbable or how far away this realization may see, or how dark the prospects may be, if we visualize them as best we can, as vividly as possible, hold tenaciously to them and vigorously struggle to attain them, they will gradually become actualized, realized in the life. But a desire, a longing without endeavor, a yearning abandoned or held indifferently will vanish without realization.

Self Help   ISBN: *1-59462-644-8*   Pages:360   MSRP *$25.45* www.bookjungle.com email: sales@bookjungle.com fax: 630-214-0564 mail: Book Jungle PO Box 2226 Champaign, IL 61825

QTY

	Title	ISBN	Price
☐	**The Rosicrucian Cosmo-Conception Mystic Christianity** by *Max Heindel* The Rosicrucian Cosmo-conception is not dogmatic, neither does it appeal to any other authority than the reason of the student. It is: not controversial, but is: sent forth in the hope that it may help to clear...	ISBN: *1-59462-188-8* New Age/Religion Pages 646	**$38.95**
☐	**Abandonment To Divine Providence** by *Jean-Pierre de Caussade* "The Rev. Jean Pierre de Caussade was one of the most remarkable spiritual writers of the Society of Jesus in France in the 18th Century. His death took place at Toulouse in 1751. His works have gone through many editions and have been republished...	ISBN: *1-59462-228-0* Inspirational/Religion Pages 400	**$25.95**
☐	**Mental Chemistry** by *Charles Haanel* Mental Chemistry allows the change of material conditions by combining and appropriately utilizing the power of the mind. Much like applied chemistry creates something new and unique out of careful combinations of chemicals the mastery of mental chemistry...	ISBN: *1-59462-192-6* New Age Pages 354	**$23.95**
☐	**The Letters of Robert Browning and Elizabeth Barret Barrett 1845-1846 vol II** by *Robert Browning* and *Elizabeth Barrett*	ISBN: *1-59462-193-4* Biographies Pages 596	**$35.95**
☐	**Gleanings In Genesis (volume I)** by *Arthur W. Pink* Appropriately has Genesis been termed "the seed plot of the Bible" for in it we have, in germ form, almost all of the great doctrines which are afterwards fully developed in the books of Scripture which follow...	ISBN: *1-59462-130-6* Religion/Inspirational Pages 420	**$27.45**
☐	**The Master Key** by *L. W. de Laurence* In no branch of human knowledge has there been a more lively increase of the spirit of research during the past few years than in the study of Psychology, Concentration and Mental Discipline. The requests for authentic lessons in Thought Control, Mental Discipline and...	ISBN: *1-59462-001-6* New Age/Business Pages 422	**$30.95**
☐	**The Lesser Key Of Solomon Goetia** by *L. W. de Laurence* This translation of the first book of the "Lemegton" which is now for the first time made accessible to students of Talismanic Magic was done, after careful collation and edition, from numerous Ancient Manuscripts in Hebrew, Latin, and French...	ISBN: *1-59462-092-X* New Age/Occult Pages 92	**$9.95**
☐	**Rubaiyat Of Omar Khayyam** by *Edward Fitzgerald* Edward Fitzgerald, whom the world has already learned, in spite of his own efforts to remain within the shadow of anonymity, to look upon as one of the rarest poets of the century, was born at Bredfield, in Suffolk, on the 31st of March, 1809. He was the third son of John Purcell...	ISBN: *1-59462-332-5* Music Pages 172	**$13.95**
☐	**Ancient Law** by *Henry Maine* The chief object of the following pages is to indicate some of the earliest ideas of mankind, as they are reflected in Ancient Law, and to point out the relation of those ideas to modern thought.	ISBN: *1-59462-128-4* Religiom/History Pages 452	**$29.95**
☐	**Far-Away Stories** by *William J. Locke* "Good wine needs no bush, but a collection of mixed vintages does. And this book is just such a collection. Some of the stories I do not want to remain buried for ever in the museum files of dead magazine-numbers an author's not unpardonable vanity..."	ISBN: *1-59462-129-2* Fiction Pages 272	**$19.45**
☐	**Life of David Crockett** by *David Crockett* "Colonel David Crockett was one of the most remarkable men of the times in which he lived. Born in humble life, but gifted with a strong will, an indomitable courage, and unremitting perseverance...	ISBN: *1-59462-250-7* Biographies/New Age Pages 424	**$27.45**
☐	**Lip-Reading** by *Edward Nitchie* Edward B. Nitchie, founder of the New York School for the Hard of Hearing, now the Nitchie School of Lip-Reading, Inc, wrote "LIP-READING Principles and Practice". The development and perfecting of this meritorious work on lip-reading was an undertaking...	ISBN: *1-59462-206-X* How-to Pages 400	**$25.95**
☐	**A Handbook of Suggestive Therapeutics, Applied Hypnotism, Psychic Science** by *Henry Munro*	ISBN: *1-59462-214-0* Health/New Age/Health/Self-help Pages 376	**$24.95**
☐	**A Doll's House: and Two Other Plays** by *Henrik Ibsen* Henrik Ibsen created this classic when in revolutionary 1848 Rome. Introducing some striking concepts in playwriting for the realist genre, this play has been studied the world over.	ISBN: *1-59462-112-8* Fiction/Classics/Plays 308	**$19.95**
☐	**The Light of Asia** by *sir Edwin Arnold* In this poetic masterpiece, Edwin Arnold describes the life and teachings of Buddha. The man who was to become known as Buddha to the world was born as Prince Gautama of India but he rejected the worldly riches and abandoned the reigns of power when...	ISBN: *1-59462-204-3* Religion/History/Biographies Pages 170	**$13.95**
☐	**The Complete Works of Guy de Maupassant** by *Guy de Maupassant* "For days and days, nights and nights, I had dreamed of that first kiss which was to consecrate our engagement, and I knew not on what spot I should put my lips..."	ISBN: *1-59462-157-8* Fiction/Classics Pages 240	**$16.95**
☐	**The Art of Cross-Examination** by *Francis L. Wellman* Written by a renowned trial lawyer, Wellman imparts his experience and uses case studies to explain how to use psychology to extract desired information through questioning.	ISBN: *1-59462-309-0* How-to/Science/Reference Pages 408	**$26.95**
☐	**Answered or Unanswered?** by *Louisa Vaughan* Miracles of Faith in China	ISBN: *1-59462-248-5* Religion Pages 112	**$10.95**
☐	**The Edinburgh Lectures on Mental Science (1909)** by *Thomas* This book contains the substance of a course of lectures recently given by the writer in the Queen Street Hall, Edinburgh. Its purpose is to indicate the Natural Principles governing the relation between Mental Action and Material Conditions...	ISBN: *1-59462-008-3* New Age/Psychology Pages 148	**$11.95**
☐	**Ayesha** by *H. Rider Haggard* Verily and indeed it is the unexpected that happens! Probably if there was one person upon the earth from whom the Editor of this, and of a certain previous history, did not expect to hear again...	ISBN: *1-59462-301-5* Classics Pages 380	**$24.95**
☐	**Ayala's Angel** by *Anthony Trollope* The two girls were both pretty, but Lucy who was twenty-one who supposed to be simple and comparatively unattractive, whereas Ayala was credited, as her Bombwhat romantic name might show, with poetic charm and a taste for romance. Ayala when her father died was nineteen...	ISBN: *1-59462-352-X* Fiction Pages 484	**$29.95**
☐	**The American Commonwealth** by *James Bryce* An interpretation of American democratic political theory. It examines political mechanics and society from the perspective of Scotsman James Bryce	ISBN: *1-59462-286-8* Politics Pages 572	**$34.45**
☐	**Stories of the Pilgrims** by *Margaret P. Pumphrey* This book explores pilgrims religious oppression in England as well as their escape to Holland and eventual crossing to America on the Mayflower, and their early days in New England...	ISBN: *1-59462-116-0* History Pages 268	**$17.95**

www.bookjungle.com *email: sales@bookjungle.com fax: 630-214-0564 mail: Book Jungle PO Box 2226 Champaign, IL 61825*

QTY

The Fasting Cure *by **Sinclair Upton***   ISBN: *1-59462-222-1*   **$13.95**
In the Cosmopolitan Magazine for May, 1910, and in the Contemporary Review (London) for April, 1910, I published an article dealing with my experiences in fasting. I have written a great many magazine articles, but never one which attracted so much attention...   New Age/Self Help/Health Pages 164

Hebrew Astrology *by **Sepharial***   ISBN: *1-59462-308-2*   **$13.45**
In these days of advanced thinking it is a matter of common observation that we have left many of the old landmarks behind and that we are now pressing forward to greater heights and to a wider horizon than that which represented the mind-content of our progenitors...   Astrology Pages 144

Thought Vibration or The Law of Attraction in the Thought World   ISBN: *1-59462-127-6*   **$12.95**
*by **William Walker Atkinson***   Psychology/Religion Pages 144

Optimism *by **Helen Keller***   ISBN: *1-59462-108-X*   **$15.95**
Helen Keller was blind, deaf, and mute since 19 months old, yet famously learned how to overcome these handicaps, communicate with the world, and spread her lectures promoting optimism. An inspiring read for everyone...   Biographies/Inspirational Pages 84

Sara Crewe *by **Frances Burnett***   ISBN: *1-59462-360-0*   **$9.45**
In the first place, Miss Minchin lived in London. Her home was a large, dull, tall one, in a large, dull square, where all the houses were alike, and all the sparrows were alike, and where all the door-knockers made the same heavy sound...   Childrens/Classic Pages 88

The Autobiography of Benjamin Franklin *by **Benjamin Franklin***   ISBN: *1-59462-135-7*   **$24.95**
The Autobiography of Benjamin Franklin has probably been more extensively read than any other American historical work, and no other book of its kind has had such ups and downs of fortune. Franklin lived for many years in England, where he was agent...   Biographies/History Pages 332

Name	
Email	
Telephone	
Address	
City, State ZIP	

☐ Credit Card   ☐ Check / Money Order

Credit Card Number	
Expiration Date	
Signature	

Please Mail to: Book Jungle
PO Box 2226
Champaign, IL 61825
or Fax to: 630-214-0564

ORDERING INFORMATION

web: *www.bookjungle.com*
email: *sales@bookjungle.com*
fax: *630-214-0564*
mail: *Book Jungle PO Box 2226 Champaign, IL 61825*
or PayPal *to sales@bookjungle.com*

Please contact us for bulk discounts

DIRECT-ORDER TERMS

**20% Discount if You Order
Two or More Books**
Free Domestic Shipping!
Accepted: Master Card, Visa,
Discover, American Express

www.ingramcontent.com/pod-product-compliance
Lightning Source LLC
Chambersburg PA
CBHW081350040426
42450CB00015B/3383